$15-

The Journal of Major George Washington

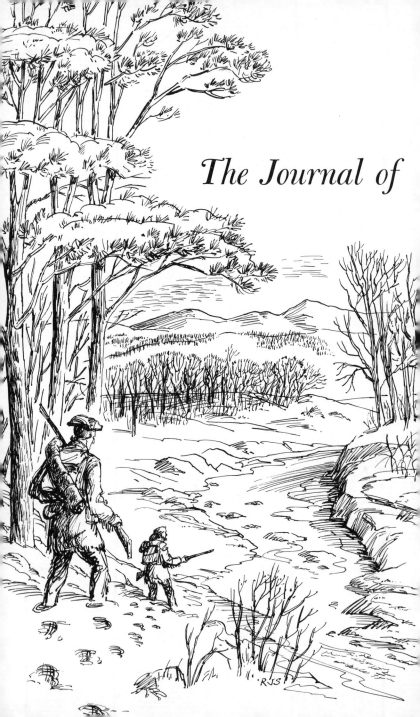

The Journal of

Major George Washington

AN ACCOUNT OF HIS FIRST OFFICIAL
MISSION, MADE AS EMISSARY FROM THE
GOVERNOR OF VIRGINIA TO THE COM-
MANDANT OF THE FRENCH FORCES ON
THE OHIO, OCTOBER 1753 - JANUARY 1754

Facsimile Edition
Published by the COLONIAL WILLIAMSBURG FOUNDATION
Williamsburg, Virginia

Library of Congress Catalogue Card No. 59-9062
Colonial Williamsburg ISBN 0-910412-57-X
FIFTH PRINTING, 1979

PRINTED IN THE UNITED STATES OF AMERICA

Introduction

At the age of twenty-one George Washington wrote a testimonial to his maturity and capacity for leadership. It can be read in the pages of the journal that follows — a report written hurriedly after he had delivered a message from Governor Dinwiddie of Virginia to the French commander in the Ohio Valley. Modest about his first effort as an author, Washington apologized at the beginning of the journal for its "numberless Imperfections" and thought it would have no more than a cursory reading. In this he was wrong. It was widely read and quoted even within weeks of publication. It continues to be read for its description of the blunt realities of frontier diplomacy in colonial America, and as a record of the first critical test of Washington's qualifications for public service.

Washington's mission was not mere routine. He was to deliver a message to the French and to obtain a reply. But this curt diplomatic exchange was a tense and urgent assignment — the kind of eleventh-hour negotiation that often precedes open hostilities. France and England, never warm neighbors in the New World, were again near

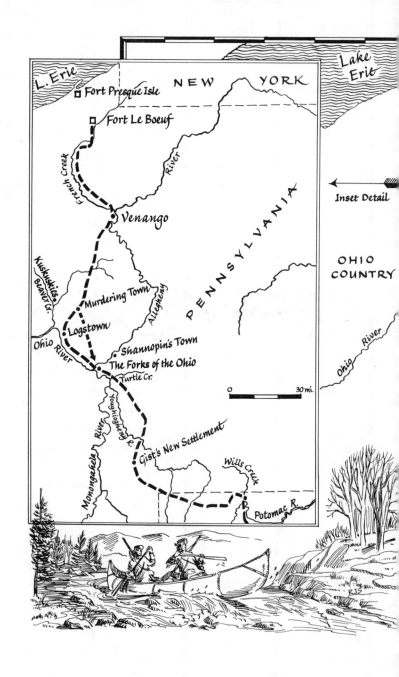

L. Erie

Fort Presque Isle

NEW YORK

Lake Erie

Fort Le Boeuf

River

French Creek

← Inset Detail

Venango

PENNSYLVANIA

OHIO COUNTRY

Kuskuskies

Beaver Cr.

Murdering Town

Allegheny

Logstown

Ohio River

Shannopin's Town

The Forks of the Ohio

Turtle Cr.

Ohio River

0   30 mi.

Youghiogheny R.

Monongahela River

Gist's New Settlement

Wills Creek

Potomac R.

RJ2

NEW YORK

Fort Le Boeuf

River

Venango

Allegheny

Ohio R.

The Forks

PENNSYLVANIA

Monongahela R.

Wills Cr.

MARYLAND

Potomac

River

Winchester

Alexandria

VIRGINIA

Fredericksburg

Rappahannock R.

Chesapeake Bay

James

River

0   50 mi.

Williamsburg

Major George Washington's Journey
1753 – 1754

the point of war. In dispute was the ownership of that enormous land area known simply as the Ohio.

In 1753 Ohio — five times larger than the present state of Virginia — was a wild, unexploited country. France had long claimed the territory, a natural link between her colonies of Canada and Louisiana, by the priority of La Salle's explorations. French traders traveling among the scattered Indian tribes who inhabited the Valley established a commerce that gave substance to the claim.

To France the Ohio Valley represented the heart of her trading empire in North America. To the colony of Virginia it was the logical frontier for expansion, while to England it was merely an unsettled part of her original claim. To be sure, the western boundary of the claim was not entirely clear either to Englishmen or Virginians. For whatever reassurance might lie in the fact, they could argue that the colony, by the charter of 1609, reached to the Pacific Ocean.

When news drifted northward that the English Ohio Company was preparing to settle the Valley, France took practical steps to tighten her grip on the region and reinforce the advantage that lay in occupation. Céloron de Blainville traveled in a wide circle south of Lake Erie, burying along the way lead plates declaring French ownership of the territory. Supply routes were established and mapped. Indian sachems were courted. Small forts began to appear at key points.

Hearing reports of these activities, the English saw

in them preparations for a colossal theft of the immediate frontier. To Dinwiddie, himself a stockholder in the Ohio Company, two facts were plain: the French must be told to get off the land, and Indian support must be won for the English claim, or at least denied to the French. Only a dependable envoy could be trusted with such an assignment. George Washington, at twenty-one already a major of Virginia militia, learned about the mission, packed away his surveyor's theodolite and plumb line, rode down to Williamsburg, and volunteered. He was appointed.

It was a delicate responsibility. The issue between France and England was clear-cut, but resentment and distrust on both sides complicated the chance for a peaceful solution. Nevertheless, both sides still insisted on the protocol of diplomacy. "I made it my particular care," the French commander wrote Dinwiddie, "to receive Mr. Washington with a distinction suitable to your dignity, and his quality and great merit."

If the amenities had to be fitted to a primitive setting, so did the contest for support of the Indian population. Here diplomacy took on its crudest form. Its trappings were rum and guns, cheap baubles and extravagant promises. Its nuances, its hidden motives, were reduced to the blunt language of the wampum belt. Washington was competing with experts. "I can't say that ever in my life," he reported of one exasperating maneuver, "I suffered so much anxiety as I did in this affair."

He acquitted himself well. If the French could buy

allies in a disputed land the technique was not theirs alone. Having paid a belated visit to Queen Alliquippa, Washington recorded with a rare touch of humor that he had "made her a present of a matchcoat and a bottle of rum, which latter was thought to be much the best present of the two."

While Washington competed for the friendship of the Indians he was careful, whenever he had the opportunity, to note the extent of French armament and offensive preparation. He had not yet acquired the eye of the experienced soldier for reconnoitering terrain, but as a surveyor he could recognize where lay the most advantageous land — valuable intelligence if diplomacy gave way to force. There is no reason to believe that Washington thought a British ultimatum would really expel the French from the Ohio. Still, should that unlikely withdrawal take place, the Ohio Company might find profit in his observations.

An even more immediate adversary than the French was the bone-chilling weather that harassed Washington throughout most of his nine-hundred-mile trip. There was no negotiation or compromise with the raw winter of western Pennsylvania. His only defense was physical hardihood. A bleak sky hid the sun; scanty forage and severe cold weakened the horses; wind-whipped rain froze to his clothes. With a shiver we read of Washington and his veteran guide Christopher Gist, fugitives from their overturned raft, floundering in the dark toward an island in the turbulent Allegheny River. Next morning escape from the island was made easy by enemy turned friend: the river had frozen over.

Poor weather accompanied Washington all the way back to Williamsburg. When he arrived in mid-January, Washington delivered his report to Dinwiddie, who promptly ordered it printed to advertise the nature of the crisis in the backcountry. This was both necessary and prudent: the Councillors and the Burgesses could thus learn of the gravity of the situation before they were asked for funds to deal with it. Dinwiddie took further measures. The April meeting of the General Assembly was rescheduled for February. Troops would be needed to protect a fort already authorized at the forks of the Allegheny and the Monongahela. More troops would be required elsewhere. Washington was commissioned a lieutenant-colonel and given the new task of raising a militia to strengthen the British claim.

Three months later, in May 1754, a volley from the muskets of Washington's militiamen opened the French and Indian war in western Pennsylvania. The struggle that followed swept France from the North American continent. Yet a generation later the Ohio Valley belonged to neither France nor England. Ownership of a land, after all, depends not upon claim but upon control. And in control of the Ohio Valley was the new United States of America.

* * * *

Contents

Facsimile

THE
JOURNAL
OF

Major *George Washington,*

SENT BY THE

Hon. *ROBERT DINWIDDIE,* Esq;
His Majesty's Lieutenant-Governor, and
Commander in Chief of *VIRGINIA,*

TO THE

COMMANDANT
OF THE

FRENCH FORCES
ON

O H I O.

TO WHICH ARE ADDED, THE

GOVERNOR's LETTER;
AND A TRANSLATION OF THE
FRENCH OFFICER's ANSWER.

═══════════════════════════════

WILLIAMSBURG:
Printed by WILLIAM HUNTER. 1754

ADVERTISEMENT.

AS it was thought adviseable by his Honour the Governor to have the following Account of my Proceedings to and from the French on Ohio, committed to Print ; I think I can do no less than apologize, in some Measure, for the numberless Imperfections of it.

There intervened but one Day between my Arrival in Williamsburg, and the Time for the Council's Meeting, for me to prepare and transcribe, from the rough Minutes I had taken in my Travels, this Journal; the writing of which only was sufficient to employ me closely the whole Time, consequently admitted of no Leisure to consult of a new and proper Form to offer it in, or to correct or amend the Diction of the old ; neither was I apprised, or did in the least conceive, when I wrote this for his Honour's Perusal, that it ever would be published, or even have more than a cursory Reading ; till I was informed, at the Meeting of the present General Assembly, that it was already in the Press.

There is nothing can recommend it to the Public, but this. Those Things which came under the Notice of my own Observation, I have been explicit and just in a Recital of :———Those which I have gathered from Report, I have been particularly cautious not to augment, but collected the Opinions of the several Intelligencers, and selected from the whole, the most probable and consistent Account.

G. WASHINGTON.

THE

JOURNAL, &c.

Wednesday, *October* 31*st*, 1753,

WAS commissioned and appointed by the Honourable *Robert Dinwiddie*, Esq; Governor, &c. of *Virginia*, to visit and deliver a Letter to the Commandant of the *French* Forces on the *Ohio*, and set out on the intended Journey the same Day ; the next, I arrived at *Fredericksburg*, and engaged Mr. *Jacob Vanbraam*, to be my *French* Interpreter ; and proceeded with him to *Alexandria*, where we provided Necessaries ; from thence we went to *Winchester*, and got Baggage, Horses, &c. and from thence we pursued the new Road to *Wills*-Creek, where we arrived the 14th of *November*.

Here I engaged Mr. *Gist* to pilot us out, and also hired four others as Servitors, *Barnaby Currin*, and *John Mac-Quire*, Indian Traders, *Henry Steward*, and *William Jenkins*, and in Company with those Persons, left the Inhabitants the Day following.

The excessive Rains and vast Quantity of Snow that had fallen, prevented our reaching Mr. *Frazier*'s an Indian Trader, at the Mouth of *Turtle*-Creek, on *Monongahela*, till *Thursday* the 22d. We were informed here, that Expresses were sent a few Days ago to the Traders down the River, to acquaint them with the *French* General's Death, and the Re-

A 2

turn of the major Part of the *French* Army into Winter Quarters.

The Waters were quite impassable, without swimming our Horses; which obliged us to get the Loan of a Canoe from *Frazier*, and to send *Barnaby Currin*, and *Henry Steward*, down *Monongahela*, with our Baggage, to meet us at the Forks of *Ohio*, about 10 Miles, to cross *Aligany*.

As I got down before the Canoe, I spent some Time in viewing the Rivers, and the Land in the Fork, which I think extremely well situated for a Fort, as it has the absolute Command of both Rivers. The Land at the Point is 20 or 25 Feet above the common Surface of the Water, and a considerable Bottom of flat, well-timbered Land all around it, very convenient for Building : The Rivers are each a Quarter of a Mile, or more, across, and run here very near at right Angles : *Aligany* bearing N. E. and *Monongahela* S. E. the former of these two is a very rapid and swift running Water, the other deep and still, without any perceptible Fall.

About two Miles from this, on the South East Side of the River, at the Place where the *Ohio* Company intended to erect a Fort, lives *Shingiss*, King of the *Delawares*; we call'd upon him, to invite him to Council at the *Loggs-Town*.

As I had taken a good deal of Notice Yesterday of the Situation at the *Forks*, my Curiosity led me to examine this more particularly, and I think it greatly inferior, either for Defence or Advantages; especially the latter; for a Fort at the *Forks* would be equally well situated on *Ohio*, and have the entire Command of *Monongahela*, which runs up to our Settlements and is extremely well design'd for Water Carriage, as it is of a deep still Nature; besides, a Fort at the *Fork* might be built at a much less Expence, than at the other Place.——

Nature has well contrived the lower Place, for Water Defence; but the Hill whereon it must stand being about a

Quarter

Quarter of a Mile in Length, and then defcending gradually on the Land Side, will render it difficult and very expenfive, making a fufficient Fortification there.——The whole Flat upon the Hill muft be taken in, or the Side next the Defcent made extremely high ; or elfe the Hill cut away : Otherwife, the Enemy may raife Batteries within that Diftance without being expos'd to a fingle Shot from the Fort.

Shingifs attended us to the *Loggs*-Town, where we arrived between Sun-fetting and Dark, the 25th Day after I left *Williamfburg :* We travelled over fome extreme good, and bad Land, to get to this Place.——

As foon as I came into Town, I went to *Monacatoocha* (as the Half-King was out at his hunting Cabbin on little *Beaver* Creek, about 15 Miles off) and inform'd him by *John Davifon* my *Indian* Interpreter, that I was fent a Meffenger to the *French* General ; and was ordered to call upon the Sachems of the *Six Nations*, to acquaint them with it.——I gave him a String of Wampum, and a Twift of Tobacco, and defired him to fend for the Half-King ; which he promifed to do by a Runner in the Morning, and for other Sachems.——I invited him and the other great Men prefent to my Tent, where they ftay'd about an Hour and return'd.

According to the beft Obfervations I could make, Mr. *Gift*'s new Settlement (which we pafs'd by) bears about W. N. W. 70 Miles from *Wills*-Creek ; *Shanapins,* or the Forks N. by W. or N. N. W. about 50 Miles from that ; and from thence to the *Loggs*-Town, the Courfe is nearly Weft about 18 or 20 Miles ; fo that the whole Diftance, as we went and computed it, is at leaft 135 or 140 Miles from our back Inhabitants.

25th, Came to Town four of ten *Frenchmen* that deferted from a Company at the *Cufcufcas,* which lies at the Mouth of this River ; I got the following Account from them. They were fent from *New Orleans* with 100 Men,

and

and 8 Canoe Loads of Provisions to this Place; where they expected to have met the same Number of Men, from the Forts this Side Lake *Erie*, to convoy them and the Stores up, who were not arrived when they ran off.

I enquired into the Situation of the *French*, on the *Mississippi*, their Number, and what Forts they had built : They inform'd me, That there were four small Forts between *New-Orleans* and the *Black-Islands*, garrison'd with about 30 or 40 Men, and a few small Pieces, in each : That at *New-Orleans*, which is near the Mouth of the *Mississippi*, there are 35 Companies, of 40 Men each, with a pretty strong Fort mounting 8 Carriage Guns ; and at the *Black-Islands* there are several Companies, and a Fort with 6 Guns. The *Black-Islands* are about 130 Leagues above the Mouth of the *Ohio*, which is about 350 above *New-Orleans* : They also acquainted me, that there was a small pallisado'd Fort on the *Ohio*, at the Mouth of the *Obaish* about 60 Leagues from the *Mississippi* : The *Obaish* heads near the West End of Lake *Erie*, and affords the Communication between the *French* on *Mississippi* and those on the Lakes. These Deserters came up from the lower *Shanoah* Town with one *Brown*, an *Indian* Trader, and were going to *Philadelphia*.

About 3 o'Clock this Evening the Half-King came to Town ; I went up and invited him and *Davison*, privately, to my Tent, and desir'd him to relate some of the Particulars of his Journey to the *French* Commandant, and Reception there ; and to give me an Account of the Ways and Distance. He told me, that the nearest and levellest Way was now impassable, by Reason of many large miry Savannas ; that we must be obliged to go by *Venango*, and should not get to the near Fort under 5 or 6 Night's Sleep, good Travelling. When he went to the Fort, he said he was received in a very stern Manner by the late Commander ; Who ask'd him very abruptly, what he had come about, and to declare his Business, which he said he did in the following Speech.

Fathers,

Fathers, I am come to tell you your own Speeches: what your own Mouths have declared. Fathers, You, in former Days, set a Silver Bason before us, wherein there was the Leg of a Beaver, and desir'd of all Nations to come and eat of it; to eat in Peace and Plenty, and not to be churlish to one another; and that if any such Person should be found to be a Disturber, I here lay down by the Edge of the Dish a Rod, which you must scourge them with; and if I your Father, should get foolish, in my old Days, I desire you may use it upon me as well as others.

Now Fathers, it is you that are the Disturbers in this Land, by coming and building your Towns, and taking it away unknown to us, and by Force.

Fathers, We kindled a Fire a long Time ago, at a Place called Montreal, *where we desired you to stay, and not to come and intrude upon our Land. I now desire you may dispatch to that Place; for be it known to you, Fathers, that this is our Land, and not yours.*

Fathers, I desire you may hear me in Civilness; if not, we must handle that Rod which was laid down for the Use of the obstreperous. If you had come in a peaceable Manner, like our Brothers the English, *we should not have been against your trading with us, as they do; but to come, Fathers, and build great Houses upon our Land, and to take it by Force, is what we cannot submit to.*

Fathers, Both you and the English *are white, we live in a Country between; therefore the Land belongs to neither one nor t'other: But the Great Being above allow'd it to be a Place of Residence for us; so Fathers, I desire you to withdraw, as I have done our Brothers the* English; *for I will keep you at Arms length: I lay this down as a Trial for both, to see which will have the greatest Regard to it, and that Side we will stand by, and make equal Sharers with us. Our Brothers the* English *have heard this, and I come now to tell it to you, for I am not afraid to discharge you off this Land.*

This

This he faid was the Subftance of what he faid to the General, who made this Reply.

Now my Child, I have heard your Speech, you fpoke firft, but it is my Time to fpeak now. Where is my Wampum that you took away, with the Marks of Towns in it? This Wampum I do not know, which you have difcharged me off the Land with; but you need not put yourfelf to the Trouble of fpeaking, for I will not hear you: I am not afraid of Flies, or Mufquitos, for Indians are fuch as thofe; I tell you, down that River I will go, and will build upon it, according to my Command: If the River was block'd up, I have Forces fufficient to burft it open, and tread under my Feet all that ftand in Oppofition, together with their Alliances; for my Force is as the Sand upon the Sea Shore: Therefore, here is your Wampum, I fling it at you. Child, you talk foolifh; you fay this Land belongs to you, but there is not the Black of my Nail yours: I faw that Land fooner than you did, before the Shannoahs and you were at War: Lead was the Man that went down, and took Poffeffion of that River: It is my Land, and I will have it, let who will ftand up for, or fay againft it. I'll buy and fell with the Englifh, (mockingly). If People will be rul'd by me, they may expect Kindnefs, but not elfe.

The Half-King told me he enquired of the General after two *Englifhmen* that were made Prifoners, and received this Anfwer,

Child, You think it is a very great Hardfhip that I made Prifoners of thofe two People at Venango, don't you concern yourfelf with it, we took and carried them to Canada, to get Intelligence of what the Englifh were doing in Virginia.

He informed me that they had built two Forts, one on Lake *Erie,* and another on *French*-Creek, near a fmall Lake about

about 15 Miles afunder, and a large Waggon Road between; they are both built after the fame Model, but different in the Size ; that on the Lake the largeft; he gave me a Plan of them, of his own drawing.

The *Indians* enquired very particularly after their Brothers in *Carolina* Goal.

They also afked what Sort of a Boy it was that was taken from the *South*-Branch; for they had, by fome *Indians*, heard that a Party of *French Indians* had carried a white Boy by the *Cufcufca* Town, towards the Lakes.

26*th.* We met in Council at the *Long-Houfe,* about 9 o' Clock, where I fpoke to them as follows,

Brothers, I have called you together in Council, by Order of your Brother the Governor of Virginia, *to acquaint you that I am fent, with all poffible Difpatch, to vifit, and deliver a Letter to the* French *Commandant, of very great Importance to your Brothers the* Englifh; *and I dare fay, to you their Friends and Allies.*

I was defired, Brothers, by your Brother the Governor, to call upon you, the Sachems of the Nations, to inform you of it, and to afk your Advice and Affiftance to proceed the neareft and beft Road to the French. *You fee, Brothers, I have got thus far on my Journey.*

His Honour likewife defired me to apply to you for fome of your young Men, to conduct and provide Provifions for us on our Way, and be a Safeguard againft thofe French Indians *who have taken up the Hatchet againft us. I have fpoke this particularly to you, Brothers, becaufe his Honour our Governor treats you as good Friends and Allies, and holds you in great Efteem. To confirm what I have faid, I give you this String of Wampum.*

After they had confidered fome Time on the above, the Half-King got up and fpoke.

Now, my Brothers, in Regard to what my Brother the Governor has defired of me, I return you this Anfwer.

I rely upon you as a Brother ought to do, as you fay we are Brothers and one People : We fhall put Heart in Hand, and fpeak to our Fathers the French *concerning the Speech they made to me, and you may depend that we will endeavour to be your Guard.*

Brother, as you have afked my Advice, I hope you will be ruled by it, and ftay till I can provide a Company to go with you : The French *Speech-Belt is not here, I have it to go for to my hunting Cabbin; likewife the People which I have ordered in, are not yet come, nor cannot till the third Night from this, till which Time, Brother, I muft beg you to ftay.*

I intend to fend a Guard of Mingo's, Shannoahs, *aud* Delawares, *that our Brothers may fee the Love and Loyalty we bear them.*

As I had Orders to make all poffible Difpatch, and waiting here was very contrary to my Inclination, I thanked him in the moft fuitable Manner I could, and told him that my Bufinefs required the greateft Expedition, and would not admit of that Delay: He was not well pleafed that I fhould offer to go before the Time he had appointed, and told me that he could not confent to our going without a Guard, for Fear fome Accident fhould befal us, and draw a Reflection upon him ; befides, fays he, this is a Matter of no fmall Moment, and muft not be entered into without due Confideration ; for now I intend to deliver up the *French*-Speech-Belt, and make the *Shanoahs* and *Delawares* do the fame : and accordingly he gave Orders to King *Shingifs*, who was prefent, to attend on *Wednefday* Night with the Wampum, and two Men of their Nation to be in Readinefs to fet out with us next Morning. As I found it was impoffible to get off without affronting them in the moft egregious Manner, I confented to ftay.

I gave

I gave them back a String of Wampum that I met with at Mr. *Frazier*'s, which they had sent with a Speech to his Honour the Governor, to inform him, that three Nations of *French Indians*, viz. *Chippoways*, *Ottoways*, and *Orundacks*, had taken up the Hatchet against the *English*, and desired them to repeat it over again, which they postponed doing till they met in full Council with the *Shannoahs* and *Delaware* Chiefs.

27*th.* Runners were dispatched very early for the *Shanoah* Chiefs, the Half-King set out himself to fetch the *French*-Speech-Belt from his Hunting-Cabbin.

28*th.* He returned this Evening, and came with *Monocatoocha*, and two other Sachems to my Tent ; and begged, (as they had complied with his Honour the Governor's Request, in providing Men, &c.) to know on what Business we were going to the *French* ? this was a Question I all along expected, and had provided as satisfactory Answers to, as I could, and which allayed their Curiosity a little.

Monocatoocha informed me, that an *Indian* from *Venango* brought News, a few Days ago, that the *French* had called all the *Mingos*, *Delawares*, &c. together at that Place, and told them that they intended to have been down the River this Fall, but the Waters were growing cold, and the Winter advancing, which obliged them to go into Quarters : But they might assuredly expect them in the Spring, with a far greater Number ; and desired that they might be quite passive, and not to intermeddle, unless they had a Mind to draw all their Force upon them, for that they expected to fight the *English* three Years, (as they supposed there would be some Attempts made to stop them) in which Time they should conquer, but if they should prove equally strong, that they and the *English*, would join to cut them all off, and divide the Land between them ; that tho' they had lost their General, and some few of their Soldiers, yet there were Men enough to reinforce them, and make them Masters of the *Ohio*.

This

This Speech, he said, was delivered to them by one Captain *Joncaire* their Interpreter in Chief, living at *Venango*, and a Man of Note in the Army.

29th. The Half-King and *Monocatoocha*, came very early, and begged me to stay one Day more, for notwithstanding they had used all the Diligence in their Power, the *Shanoah* Chiefs had not brought the Wampum they ordered, but would certainly be in To-night; if not, they would delay me no longer, but would send it after us as soon as they arrived: When I found them so pressing in their Request, and knew that returning of Wampum was the abolishing of Agreements; and giving this up, was shaking of all Dependence upon the *French*, I consented to stay, as I believed an Offence offered at this Crisis, might be attended with greater ill Consequence, than another Day's Delay. They also informed me that *Shingiss* could not get in his Men, and was prevented from coming himself by his Wife's Sickness, (I believe, by Fear of the *French*) but that the Wampum of that Nation was lodged with *Custaloga* one of their Chiefs at *Venango*.

In the Evening late they came again and acquainted me that the *Shannoahs* were not yet come, but it should not retard the Prosecution of our Journey. He delivered in my Hearing, the Speeches that were to be made to the *French*, by *Jeskakake*, one of their old Chiefs, which was giving up the Belt the late Commandant had asked for, and repeating near the same Speech he himself had done before.

He also delivered a String of Wampum to this Chief, which was sent by King *Shingiss*, to be given to *Custaloga*, with Orders to repair to the *French*, and deliver up the Wampum.

He likewise gave a very large String of black and white Wampum, which was to be sent up immediately to the Six Nations, if the *French* refused to quit the Land at this Warning; which was the third and last Time, and was the Right of this *Jeskakake* to deliver.

30th. Last

30th. Laſt Night the great Men aſſembled to their Council-Houſe, to conſult further about this Journey, and who were to go; the Reſult of which was, that only three of their Chiefs, with one of their beſt Hunters, ſhould be our Convoy: The Reaſon which they gave for not ſending more, after what had been propoſed at Council the 26th, was, that a greater Number might give the *French* Suſpicions of ſome bad Deſign, and cauſe them to be treated rudely: But I rather think they could not get their Hunters in.

We ſet out about 9 o'Clock with the Half-King, *Jeſkakake*, *White Thunder*, and the Hunter, and travelled on the Road to *Venango*, where we arrived the 4th of *December*, without any Thing remarkable happening but a continued Series of bad Weather.

This is an old *Indian* Town, ſituated at the Mouth of *French* Creek on *Ohio*, and lies near N. about 60 Miles from the *Loggs*-Town, but more than 70 the Way we were obliged to go.

We found the *French* Colours hoiſted at a Houſe which they drove Mr. *John Frazier*, an *Engliſh* Subject, from; I immediately repaired to it, to know where the Commander reſided: There were three Officers, one of whom, Capt. *Joncaire*, inform'd me, that he had the Command of the *Ohio*, but that there was a General Officer at the near Fort, which he adviſed me to for an Anſwer. He invited us to ſup with them, and treated us with the greateſt Complaiſance.

The Wine, as they doſed themſelves pretty plentifully with it, ſoon baniſhed the Reſtraint which at firſt appear'd in their Converſation, and gave a Licenſe to their Tongues to reveal their Sentiments more freely.

They told me, That it was their abſolute Deſign to take Poſſeſſion of the *Ohio*, and by G— they would do it; for that they were ſenſible the *Engliſh* could raiſe two Men for their one; yet they knew, their Motions were too ſlow and dilatory to prevent any Undertaking of theirs. They pretend to have an undoubted Right to the River, from a Diſcovery

Difcovery made by one *La Sol* 60 Years ago; and the Rife of this Expedition is, to prevent our fettling on the River or Waters of it, as they have heard of fome Families moving out in Order thereto. From the beft Intelligence I could get, there have been 1500 Men on this Side *Ontario* Lake, but upon the Death of the General all were recalled to about 6 or 700, who were left to garrifon four Forts, 150 or there abouts in each, the firft ot which is on *French* Creek, near a fmall Lake, about 60 Miles from *Venango,* near N. N. W. the next lies on Lake *Erie,* where the greateft Part of their Stores are kept, about 15 Miles from the other; from that it is 120 Miles to the carrying Place, at the Falls of Lake *Erie,* where there is a fmall Fort which they lodge their Goods at, in bringing them from *Montreal,* the Place that all their Stores come from : The next Fort lies about 20 Miles from this, on *Ontario* Lake; between this Fort and *Montreal* there are three others, the firft of which is near oppofite to the *Englifh* Fort *Ofwego.* From the Fort on Lake *Erie* to *Montreal* is about 600 Miles, which they fay requires no more, if good Weather, than four Weeks Voyage, if they go in Barks or large Veffels, that they can crofs the Lake; but if they come in Canoes it will require 5 or 6 Weeks, for they are oblig'd to keep under the Shore.

5*th*, Rain'd exceffively all Day, which prevented our Travelling. Capt. *Joncaire* fent for the Half-King, as he had but juft heard that he came with me : He affected to be much concern'd that I did not make free to bring them in before ; I excufed it in the beft Manner I was capable, and told him I did not think their Company agreeable, as I had heard him fay a good deal in Difpraife of *Indians* in general ; but another Motive prevented me from bringing them into his Company; I knew he was Interpreter, and a Perfon of very great Influence among the *Indians*, and had lately ufed all poffible Means to draw them over to their In-

tereft;

tereſt; therefore I was deſirous of giving no Opportunity that could be avoided.

When they came in, there was great Pleaſure expreſs'd at ſeeing them; he wonder'd how they could be ſo near without coming to viſit him, made ſeveral trifling Preſents, and applied Liquor ſo faſt, that they were ſoon render'd incapable of the Buſineſs they came about, notwithſtanding the Caution that was given.

6th, The Half-King came to my Tent, quite ſober, and inſiſted very much that I ſhould ſtay and hear what he had to ſay to the *French*; I fain would have prevented his ſpeaking any Thing, 'til he came to the Commandant; but could not prevail: He told me, that at this Place a Council Fire was kindled, where all their Buſineſs with theſe People was to be tranſacted, and that the Management of the *Indian* Affairs was left ſolely to Monſieur *Joncaire*. As I was deſirous of knowing the Iſſue of this, I agreed to ſtay, but ſent our Horſes a little Way up *French* Creek, to raft over and encamp; which I knew would make it near Night.

About 10 o'Clock they met in Council; the King ſpoke much the ſame as he had before done to the General, and offer'd the *French* Speech-Belt which had before been demanded, with the Marks of four Towns on it, which Monſieur *Joncaire* refuſed to receive; but deſired him to carry it to the Fort to the Commander.

7th, Monſieur *La Force*, Commiſſary of the *French* Stores, and three other Soldiers came over to accompany us up. We found it extremely difficult getting the *Indians* off To-day, as every Stratagem had been uſed to prevent their going up with me: I had laſt Night left *John Daviſon* (the *Indian* Interpreter that I brought from the *Loggs*-Town with me) ſtrictly charg'd not to be out of their Company, as I could not get them over to my Tent (they having ſome Buſineſs with *Cuſtaloga*, to know the Reaſon why he did not deliver up the *French* Belt which he had in Keeping)
but

but was obliged to send Mr. *Gift* over To-day to fetch them, which he did with great Perfuafion.

At 11 o'Clock we fet out for the Fort, and were prevented from arriving there 'til the 11th by exceffive Rains, Snows, and bad Travelling, through many Mires and Swamps, which we were obliged to pafs, to avoid croffing the Creek, which was impoffible, either by fording or rafting, the Water was fo high and rapid.

We paffed over much good Land fince we left *Venango*, and through feveral extenfive and very rich Meadows ; one of which I believe was near four Miles in Length, and confiderably wide in fome Places.

12*th*, I prepar'd early to wait upon the Commander, and was received and conducted to him by the fecond Officer in Command ; I acquainted him with my Bufinefs, and offer'd my Commiffion and Letter, both of which he defired me to keep 'til the Arrival of Monfieur *Riparti*, Captain, at the next Fort, who was fent for and expected every Hour.

This Commander is a Knight of the military Order of St. *Lewis*, and named *Legardeur de St. Piere.* He is an elderly Gentleman, and has much the Air of a Soldier ; he was fent over to take the Command, immediately upon the Death of the late General, and arrived here about feven Days before me.

At 2 o'Clock the Gentleman that was fent for arrived, when I offer'd the Letter, *&c.* again ; which they receiv'd, and adjourn'd into a private Apartment for the Captain to tranflate, who underftood a little *Englifh* ; after he had done it, the Commander defired I would walk in, and bring my Interpreter to perufe and correct it, which I did.

13*th*, The chief Officers retired, to hold a Council of War, which gave me an Opportunity of taking the Dimenfions of the Fort, and making what Obfervations I could.

It

It is situated on the South, or West Fork of *French* Creek, near the Water, and is almost surrounded by the Creek, and a small Branch of it which forms a Kind of an Island; four Houses compose the Sides; the Bastions are made of Piles driven into the Ground, and about 12 Feet above, and sharp at Top, with Port-Holes cut for Cannon and Loop-Holes for the small Arms to fire through; there are eight 6 lb. Pieces mounted, two in each Bastion, and one Piece of four Pound before the Gate; in the Bastions are a Guard-House, Chapel, Doctor's Lodging, and the Commander's private Store, round which are laid Plat-Forms for the Cannon and Men to stand on : There are several Barracks without the Fort, for the Soldiers Dwelling, covered, some with Bark, and some with Boards, and made chiefly of Loggs: There are also several other Houses, such as Stables, Smiths Shop, &c.

I could get no certain Account of the Number of Men here; but according to the best Judgment I could form, there are an Hundred exclusive of Officers, of which there are many. I also gave Orders to the People that were with me, to take an exact Account of the Canoes that were haled up to convey their Forces down in the Spring, which they did, and told 50 of Birch Bark, and 170 of Pine, besides many others that were block'd out, in Readiness to make.

14*th*, As the Snow encreased very fast, and our Horses daily became weaker, I sent them off unloaded, under the Care of *Barnaby Currin* and two others, to make all convenient Dispatch to *Venango*, and there wait our Arrival if there was a Prospect of the Rivers freezing, if not, then to continue down to *Shanapin*'s Town, at the Forks of *Ohio*, and there to wait 'til we came to cross *Aligany*, intending myself to go down by Water, as I had the Offer of a Canoe or Two.

As I found many Plots concerted to retard the *Indians* Business, and prevent their returning with m ; I endeavour'd all that lay in my Power to frustrate their Schemes, and

B   hurry,

hurry them on to execute their intended Defign ; they accordingly preffed for Admittance this Evening, which at Length was granted them, privately, with the Commander and one or two other Officers : The Half-King told me, that he offer'd the Wampum to the Commander, who evaded taking it, and made many fair Promifes of Love and Friendfhip ; faid he wanted to live in Peace, and trade amicably with them, as a Proof of which he would fend fome Goods immediately down to the *Loggs*-Town for them ; but I rather think the Defign of that is, to bring away all our ftraggling Traders they meet with, as I privately underftood they intended to carry an Officer, *&c.* with them; and what rather confirms this Opinion, I was enquiring of the Commander, by what Authority he had made Prifoners of feveral of our *Englifh* Subjects ; he told me that the Country belong'd to them, that no *Englifhman* had a Right to trade upon thofe Waters ; and that he had Orders to make every Perfon Prifoner that attempted it on the *Ohio*, or the Waters of it.

I enquir'd of Capt. *Riparti* about the Boy that was carried by, as it was done while the Command devolved on him, between the Death of the late General, and the Arrival of the prefent ; he acknowledged, that a Boy had been carried paft, and that the *Indians* had two or three white Men's Scalps, (I was told by fome of the *Indians* at *Venango* Eight) but pretended to have forgot the Name of the Place that the Boy came from, and all the Particulars, though he -queftion'd him for fome Hours, as they were carrying him paft: I likewife enquired what they had done with *John Trotter* and *James MacClocklan*, two *Pennfylvania* Traders, whom they had taken, with all their Goods : They told me, that they had been fent to *Canada*, but were now returned Home.

This Evening I received an Anfwer to his Honour the Governor's Letter from the Commandant.

15*th*, The Commandant ordered a plentiful Store of Liquor, Provision, &c. to be put on Board our Canoe, and appeared to be extremely complaisant, though he was exerting every Artifice that he could invent . to set our own *Indians* at Variance with us, to prevent their going 'til after our Departure : Presents, Rewards, and every Thing that could be suggested by him or his Officers.——I can't say that ever in my Life I suffer'd so much Anxiety as I did in this Affair ; I saw that every Stratagem that the most fruitful Brain could invent, was practised, to win the Half-King to their Interest, and that leaving Him here was giving them the Opportunity they aimed at.——I went to the Half-King, and press'd him in the strongest Terms to go : He told me the Commandant would not discharge him 'til the Morning. I then went to the Commandant, and desired him to do their Business, and complain d of ill Treatment ; for keeping them, as they were Part of my Company, was detaining me ; which he promised not to do, but to forward my Journey as much as he could : He protested he did not keep them, but was ignorant of the Cause of their Stay ; though I soon found it out :—He had promised them a Present of Guns, &c. if they would wait 'til the Morning.

As I was very much press'd, by the *Indians*, to wait this Day for them, I consented, on a Promise, That nothing should hinder them in the Morning.

16*th.* The *French* were not slack in their Inventions to keep the Indians this Day also ; but as they were obligated, according to Promise, to give the Present, they then endeavoured to try the Power of Liquor, which I doubt not would have prevailed at any other Time than this, but I urged and insisted with the King so closely upon his Word, that he refrained, and set off with us as he had engaged.

We had a tedious and very fatiguing Passage down the Creek, several Times we had like to have been staved against Rocks, and many Times were obliged all Hands to get out

and

and remain in the Water Half an Hour or more, getting over the Shoals; at one Place the Ice had lodged and made it impaſſable by Water; therefore we were obliged to carry our Canoe acroſs a Neck of Land, a Quarter of a Mile over. We did not reach *Venango*, till the 22d, where we met with our Horſes.

This Creek is extremely crooked, I dare ſay the Diſtance between the Fort and *Venango* can't be leſs than 130 Miles, to follow the Meanders.

23d. When I got Things ready to ſet off, I ſent for the Half-King, to know whether he intended to go with us, or by Water, he told me that *White-Thunder* had hurt himſelf much, and was ſick and unable to walk, therefore he was obliged to carry him down in a Canoe: As I found he intended to ſtay here a Day or two, and knew that Monſieur *Joncaire* would employ every Scheme to ſet him againſt the *Engliſh* as he had before done; I told him I hoped he would guard againſt his Flattery, and let no fine Speeches influence him in their Favour: He deſired I might not be concerned, for he knew the *French* too well, for any Thing to engage him in their Behalf, and though he could not go down with us, he would endeavour to meet at the Forks with *Joſeph Campbell*, to deliver a Speech for me to carry to his Honour the Governor. He told me he would order the young Hunter to attend us, and get Proviſion, &c. if wanted.

Our Horſes were now ſo weak and feeble, and the Baggage heavy, as we here obliged to provide all the Neceſſaries that the Journey would require; that we doubted much their performing it: therefore myſelf and others (except the Drivers which were obliged to ride) gave up our Horſes for Packs, to aſſiſt along with the Baggage; I put myſelf in an Indian walking Dreſs, and continued with them three Days, till I found there was no Probability of their getting in, in any reaſonable Time; the Horſes grew leſs able to travel every Day; the Cold increaſed very faſt, and the Roads were becoming much worſe by a deep Snow, continually freez-

ing;

ing; and as I was uneasy to get back, to make Report of my Proceedings to his Honour the Governor, I determined to prosecute my Journey the nearest Way through the Woods, on Foot.

Accordingly I left Mr. *Vanbraam* in Charge of our Baggage, with Money and Directions, to provide Necessaries from Place to Place for themselves and Horses, and to make the most convenient Dispatch in.

I took my necessary Papers, pulled off my Cloaths; tied myself up in a Match Coat; and with my Pack at my Back with my Papers and Provisions in it, and a Gun, set out with Mr. *Gist*, fitted in the same Manner, on *Wednesday* the 26th. The Day following, just after we had passed a Place called the *Murdering*-Town, where we intended to quit the Path, and steer across the Country for *Shannapins* Town, we fell in with a Party of *French* Indians, who had lain in Wait for us; one of them fired at Mr. *Gist* or me, not 15 Steps, but fortunately missed. We took this Fellow into Custody, and kept him till about 9 o'Clock at Night, and then let him go, and walked all the remaining Part of the Night without making any Stop, that we might get the Start, so far, as to be out of the Reach of their Pursuit the next Day, as we were well assured they would follow our Tract as soon as it was light: The next Day we continued travelling till quite dark, and got to the River about two Miles above *Shannapins*; we expected to have found the River frozen, but it was not, only about 50 Yards from each Shore; the Ice I suppose had broke up above, for it was driving in vast Quantities.

There was no Way for getting over but on a Raft, which we set about, with but one poor Hatchet, and got finished just after Sun-setting, after a whole Days Work; we got it launched, and on Board of it, and set off; but before we were Half Way over, we were jammed in the Ice in such a Manner that we expected every Moment our Raft to sink, and ourselves to perish; I put out my setting Pole to try to stop the

the Raft, that the Ice might paſs by, when the Rapidity of the Stream threw it with ſo much Violence againſt the Pole, that it jirked me out into ten Feet Water, but I fortunately ſaved myſelf by catching hold of one of the Raft Logs; notwithſtanding all our Efforts we could not get the Raft to either Shore, but were obliged, as we were near an Iſland, to quit our Raft and make to it.

The Cold was ſo extremely ſevere, that Mr. *Giſt*, had all his Fingers, and ſome of his Toes frozen, and the Water was ſhut up ſo hard, that we found no Difficulty in getting off the Iſland, on the Ice, in the Morning, and went to Mr. *Frazier*'s. We met here with 20 Warriors who were going to the *Southward* to War, but coming to a Place upon the Head of the great *Cunnaway*, where they found ſeven People killed and ſcalped, all but one Woman with very light Hair, they turned about and ran back, for Fear the Inhabitants ſhould riſe and take them as the Authors of the Murder : They report that the People were lying about the Houſe, and ſome of them much torn and eaten by Hogs : By the Marks that were left, they ſay they were *French* Indians of the *Ottoway* Nation, &c. that did it.

As we intended to take Horſes here, and it required ſome Time to find them, I went up about three Miles to the Mouth of *Yaughyaughgane* to viſit Queen *Alliquippa*, who had expreſſed great Concern that we paſſed her in going to the Fort. I made her a Preſent of a Matchcoat and a Bottle of Rum, which latter was thought much the beſt Preſent of the two.

Tueſday the 1ſt Day of *January*, we left Mr. *Frazier*'s Houſe, and arrived at Mr. *Giſt*'s at *Monongahela* the 2d, where I bought Horſe, Saddle, &c. the 6th we met 17 Horſes loaded with Materials and Stores for a Fort at the Forks of *Ohio*, and the Day after ſome Families going out to ſettle: This Day we arrived at *Wills*-Creek, after as fatiguing a Journey as it is poſſible to conceive, rendered ſo by exceſſive bad Weather: From the firſt Day of *December* to the 15th, there

there was but one Day but it rained or fnowed inceffantly; and throughout the whole Journey we met with nothing but one continued Series of cold wet Weather, which occafioned very uncomfortable Lodgings, efpecially after we had left our Tent, which was fome Screen from the Inclemency of it.

On the 11th I got to *Belvoir* where I ftopped one Day to take neceffary Reft, and then fet out, and arrived in *Williamsburg* the 16th, and waited upon his Honour the Go-ernor with the Letter I had brought from the *French* Commandant, and to give an Account of the Proceedings of my Journey, which I beg Leave to do by offering the forego-ing, as it containsthe moft remarkable Occurences that hap-pened to me.

I hope it will be fufficient to fatisfy your Honour with my Proceedings; for that was my Aim in undertaking the Journey, and chief Study throughout the Profecution of it.

With the Hope of doing it, I, with infinite Pleafure, fub-fcribe myfelf,

Your Honour's moft Obedient,

And very humble Servant,

G. Wafhington.

COPY

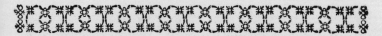

COPY of his Honour the GOVERNOR's Letter to the Commandant of the *French* Forces on the OHIO, sent by Major *Washington*.

S I R,

T H E *Lands upon the River* Ohio, *in the West-ern Parts of the Colony of* Virginia, *are so notoriously known to be the Property of the Crown of* Great-Britain, *that it is a Matter of equal* Concern *and* Surprize *to me, to hear that a Body of* French *Forces are erecting Fortresses, and making Settlements upon that River, within his Majesty's Dominions.*

The many and repeated Complaints I have received of these Acts of Hostility, lay me under the Necessity, of sending, in the Name of the King my Master, the Bearer hereof, George Washington, *Esq; one of the Adjutants General of the Forces of this Dominion, to complain to you of the Encroachments thus made, and of the Injuries done to the Subjects of* Great-Britain, *in open Violation of the Law of Nations, and the Treaties now subsisting between the two Crowns.*

If these Facts are true, and you shall think fit to justify your Proceedings, I must desire you to acquaint me, by whose Authority and Instructions you have lately marched from

C   Canada,

Canada, *with an armed Force, and invaded the King of* Great-Britain's *Territories, in the Manner complained of* ; *that according to the Purport and Resolution of your Answer, I may act agreably to the Commission I am honoured with, from the King my Master.*

However Sir, in Obedience to my Instructions, it becomes my Duty to require your peaceable Departure ; *and that you would forbear prosecuting a Purpose so interruptive of the Harmony and good Understanding, which his Majesty is desirous to continue and cultivate with the most Christian King.*

I persuade myself you will receive and entertain Major Washington *with the Candour and Politeness natural to your Nation* ; *and it will give me the greatest Satisfaction, if you return him with an Answer suitable to my Wishes for a very long and lasting Peace between us. I have the Honour to subscribe myself,*

S I R,

Your most obedient,

Humble Servant,

ROBERT DINWIDDIE.

Williamsburg, *in* Virginia,
October 31st, 1753.

TRANS-

TRANSLATION of a Letter from Mr.
Legardeur de St. Piere, a principal *French* Officer, in Anſwer to the Governor's Letter.

S I R,

*A*S I have the Honour of commanding here in
Chief, Mr. Waſhington *delivered me the Let-
ter which you writ to the Commandant of the*
French *Troops.*

*I ſhould have been glad that you had given him Or-
ders, or that he had been inclined to proceed to* Canada,
*to ſee our General, to whom it better belongs than to me
to ſet forth the Evidence and Reality of the Rights of the
King, my Maſter, upon the Lands ſituated along the
River* Ohio, *and to conteſt the Pretenſions of the King
of* Great-Britain *thereto.*

I ſhall tranſmit your Letter to the Marquiſs Duguiſne;
*his Anſwer will be a Law to me, and if he ſhall order
me to communicate it to you, Sir, you may be aſſured I
ſhall not fail to diſpatch it to you forthwith.*

*As to the Summons you ſend me to retire, I do not
think myſelf obliged to obey it ; whatever may be your
Inſtructions, I am here by* Virtue *of the Orders of my
General ; and I intreat you, Sir, not to doubt one Moment, but that I am determin'd to conform myſelf to
them with all the Exactneſs and Reſolution which can
be expected from the beſt Officer.*

I don't

I don't know that in the Progreſs of this Campaign any Thing has paſſed which can be reputed an Act of Hoſtility, or that is contrary to the Treaties which ſubſiſt between the two Crowns, the Continuation whereof as much intereſts, and is as pleaſing to us, as the English. *Had you been pleaſed, Sir, to have deſcended to particularize the Facts which occaſioned your Complaint, I ſhould have had the Honour of anſwering you in the fulleſt, and, I am perſuaded, moſt ſatisfactory Manner.*

I made it my particular Care to receive Mr. Washington, *with a Diſtinction ſuitable to your Dignity, and his Quality and great Merit ; I flatter myſelf he will do me this Juſtice before you, Sir, and that he will ſignify to you as well as I, the profound Reſpect with which I am,*

S I R,

Your moſt humble, and

moſt obedient Servant,

LEGARDEUR DE ST. PIERE.

From the Fort *ſur La Riviere au Beuf,* the 15th of *December* 1753.

Notes

Notes

PAGE 3

I was commissioned . . . to visit and deliver a Letter to the Commandant of the French Forces on the Ohio, . . . This letter appears on pages 25-26 of the journal.

Jacob Vanbraam. Van Braam was a native of Holland who came to the Fredericksburg area in 1752 from Annapolis. He had advertised in the *Maryland Gazette* of July 30, 1752, as a teacher of French. Van Braam also claimed to have been a lieutenant in the Dutch army. He was to have an important role as Washington's interpreter on the Fort Necessity expedition later in 1754.

Wills-Creek. This Ohio Company post was later known as Fort Cumberland and was on the site of the present city of Cumberland, Maryland.

Mr. Gist. Christopher Gist was an experienced frontiersman and guide for the Ohio Company. Governor Dinwiddie sent a letter by Washington requesting Gist to accompany the young Major to the French forts. Like Washington, Gist kept a journal — the only other detailed record of the expedition.

Mr. Frazier's. The Indian trading post at the mouth of Turtle Creek, which Washington reached on November 22, was operated by John Frazier, or Fraser. Besides keeping a store, Frazier operated a blacksmith's shop in which he re-

33

paired guns and tools for frontiersmen and Indians. His post had earlier stood further north at Venango, until the French expelled him.

French General's Death. The Commandant of the French forces in the Ohio area had been Pierre Paul, Sieur de Marin. This was news of some importance, since Washington would have delivered Dinwiddie's warning to this man.

PAGE 4

As I got down . . . That is, Washington reached the Forks of the Ohio.

I spent some Time in viewing the Rivers, and the Land in the Fork, . . . This is, of course, the present-day site of Pittsburgh's Golden Triangle. Washington's estimate of the strategic value of the forks of Ohio is interesting. The site became, in fact, a pivotal point in the French and Indian War, occupied first by the French Fort Duquesne and then by the English Fort Pitt.

Shingiss, King of the Delawares. This chief's name was usually spelled Shingas. He lived about two miles below the forks of the Ohio on the site of modern McKees Rocks, Pennsylvania. Shingas was a British ally; although he went over to the French after Washington's later defeat at Fort Necessity, he returned to his British allegiance after the war.

The Loggs-Town. Logstown, a well-known Indian settlement inhabited by several tribes, was located about eighteen miles down the Ohio from the forks, near the modern town of Economy, Pennsylvania. Logstown was a center for trade and diplomacy with the Indians of the upper Ohio, and Washington was able to conduct practically all of his negotiations with the Indians there.

. . . my Curiosity led me to examine this more particularly, . . . Having already inspected the ground at the forks, Washington now looked carefully over the site of Shingas' settlement where the Ohio Company originally intended to

build a fort. Washington realized the superiority of the location at the forks; but so had others. On January 6, 1754, while on the return journey to Williamsburg, Washington recorded (page 22) meeting an expedition with seventeen horses loaded with materials for "a Fort at the Forks of *Ohio*."

PAGE 5

Monacatoocha. This chief was a member of the Oneida tribe who was sent by the Council of the Six Nations to exercise authority over the Shawnees. In the Anglo-French rivalry for the Ohio area he never deviated from loyalty to the English.

The Half-King. The most important of the chiefs with whom Washington established contact, the Half-King was a Seneca and the principal representative of the Iroquois among the Ohio Indians. His tribal name was Tanacharison or Tanacharistòn, but the English referred to him as the Half-King because of his dependence on the Council of the Six Nations. Traditionally an enemy of the French, as subsequent passages of the journal clearly show, the Half-King has been described as intelligent, brave, and possessed of an unusual knowledge of the white man.

John Davison. Davison was an experienced Indian trader and interpreter, skilled in the Indian dialects of the region. Washington evidently hired him at Logstown, although the journal does not definitely say this.

Sachems. A sachem was simply an Indian chief. The word is of Algonquian origin and at first denoted the chief of a confederation.

Six Nations. The Six Nations were an Iroquoian confederacy located in central and western New York. By virtue of their superior organization they had become the dominant Indian group throughout a much larger territory, and so it was that chiefs like the Half-King and Monacatoocha were their agents in the Ohio country.

Mr. Gist's new Settlement. A settlement near present-day

Mount Braddock, Pennsylvania, established by Christopher Gist. Only one family other than Gist's had settled there when Washington and his party stopped for the night of November 18.

Shanapins. Also known as Shannopin's Town, this was a Delaware village on the Allegheny River about two miles above its junction with the Monongahela.

Came to Town four of ten Frenchmen that deserted from a Company at the Cuscuscas, . . . Hugh Cleland, *George Washington in the Ohio Valley* (Pittsburgh, 1955), pp. 47-48, argues convincingly that these deserters had come from Kaskaskia, the French settlement on the Mississippi near the mouth of the Ohio. It was earlier believed to refer to the Indian town of Kuskuskies, now New Castle, Pennsylvania, which was much closer to Logstown, but in the wrong direction, if the Frenchmen were on their way to Philadelphia.

PAGE 6

Black-Islands. This would be *Isles Noires* in French and undoubtedly represents an error in translation of *Illinois.*

The Obaish. The Wabash River. There was no fort at its mouth, but the French did have a post upstream at Vincennes.

The lower Shanoah Town. Shanoah later came to be spelled in English as Shawnee. Although there were two Shawnee settlements with the name of the Lower Town, this would logically refer to one that stood near the modern site of Portsmouth, Ohio.

The French Commandant. The officer whom the Half-King had seen was the now-deceased Sieur de Marin. As Washington's account subsequently indicated, his successor was much more diplomatic in his dealings with the Indians, a fact that was to cause the young Virginian much difficulty.

. . . many large miry Savannas; . . . A savanna was an open, level area. Those which lay on the usual route to the French forts had been made swampy by the overflow of

streams; hence the Half-King recommended the route by Venango.

Venango. Now the site of Franklin, Pennsylvania, Venango had been the location of John Frazier's earlier trading post from which the French had ousted him. Washington found it still occupied by the French.

PAGE 8

Lead. This was probably a reference to Céloron de Blainville who traveled through the Ohio Country in 1749 burying lead plates on which were recorded the French claim to the region.

. . . two Forts, one on Lake Erie, and another on French-Creek, . . . The two French forts were Fort Presque Isle, on Lake Erie at the present location of the city of Erie, and Fort LeBoeuf, at what is now Waterford, Pennsylvania. Washington's journey in 1753 took him as far as Fort LeBoeuf.

PAGE 9

Long-House. This was the usual Indian name for a building used for councils and, among some tribes, for other ceremonials and entertainments.

PAGE 10

. . . a Guard of Mingo's, Shannoahs, and Delawares, . . . Mingo was a name for the Iroquois in the Ohio Valley; the Mingos were originally Senecas. At the time of Washington's trip the Shannoahs, or Shawnees, centered along the north bank of the Ohio between the Allegheny and Scioto rivers. The Delawares originally lived along the eastern seaboard — Penn's famous treaty was signed with them — but they had been gradually pushed westward. By the 1750s they were moving into eastern Ohio.

PAGE 11

I gave them back a String of Wampum that I met with at Mr. Frazier's, . . . Washington's journal contains many references that illustrate the symbolic importance of wampum for the Indians on all such occasions as the conclusion of a treaty, presentation of a speech, etc. In this instance Washington referred to the fact that he had received at Frazier's trading post, presumably for delivery to Dinwiddie, a string of wampum that the Indians had sent with the news of an uprising of three pro-French tribes against the British. Perhaps Washington believed that if he returned the wampum to the Indians at this point in his negotiations, and asked them to repeat their speech to Dinwiddie, it would remind them of the hostile intentions of the French and influence them to support his own mission more willingly.

PAGE 12

Captain Joncaire. Philippe Thomas Joncaire was the son of a man who had also been a successful Indian agent for the French. The younger Joncaire was an adopted member of the Seneca tribe, which has been responsible for the erroneous belief that he was half Indian. He held great influence among the natives.

Custaloga. A Delaware chief then living at Venango. Shingas, to all appearances afraid of offending the French, sought to have another chief bear the onus of returning the treaty belt.

PAGE 13

Jeskakake, White Thunder, and the Hunter. No other record appears of the two Indian chiefs who accompanied the Half-King and Washington. The hunter has been identified by Hugh Cleland, *George Washington in the Ohio Valley,* p. 50, as Kiashuta or Guyasutha, who later became an Iroquois chief and fought against the English during both the French and Indian War and Pontiac's uprising.

PAGE 14

La Sol. Clearly a reference to the explorer La Salle.

. . . four Forts . . . the English Fort Oswego. The system of forts here described by Washington began with Fort

LeBoeuf and Fort Presque Isle, which have already been mentioned. The next fort, described as located 120 miles away at the Falls of Lake Erie, or Niagara Falls, was Fort Niagara. The fourth one was Fort Toronto. Standing nearly opposite to the English Fort Oswego was Fort Frontenac.

PAGE 16

Monsieur Riparti. Washington's spelling of Sieur de Repentigny, commander of Fort Presque Isle. The French desired his presence because he knew enough English to act as translator.

Legardeur de St. Piere. A veteran officer, Legardeur de St. Pierre had seen service in the upper Ohio as early as 1739. He assumed command of French forces in the area only a week before Washington arrived at Fort LeBoeuf.

PAGE 20

[December 17-22] Washington made no entries in his journal for the days between December 17 and 22, which covered the return journey from Fort LeBoeuf to Venango. Christopher Gist briefly described this period in his account. After some anxious moments spent in persuading the Indians to leave, Washington's party set out by canoe for Venango. Washington and Gist did not travel with the Indians, although they camped with them on the seventeenth and again on the twenty-first. The trip was a difficult one. The water level in the rivers and creeks was falling and threatened to become too low to float the canoes. Ice also became a problem, and once, on December 21, Washington and Gist had to carry their canoe overland for a quarter mile to avoid a place where the stream was frozen hard. On the next day, the twenty-second, the two men and the Indians, who had overtaken them the previous day, reached Joncaire's post. With the preparation for departure from Venango, Washington resumed his account.

... *he would endeavour to meet at the Forks with Joseph Campbell, to deliver a Speech for me to carry to his Honour the Governor.* Washington did not explain where he was expected to meet Campbell, who was probably an Indian trader; nor does it appear from later entries that he did so.

PAGE 21

Match Coat. An outercoat of matching skins, or sometimes of fur or wool.

The Murdering-Town. No modern city marks the location of this place roughly north of Pittsburgh, nor has the origin of its name been established. Just beyond it Washington and Gist struck out overland for Shannopin's Town and Frazier's post.

. . . we fell in with a Party of French Indians, . . . Gist gave a somewhat different account of the attempt of the Indian to kill the two men, in which he did not suggest the Indian was part of a band of French Indians or that he had deliberately waited for them.

PAGE 22

The Head of the great Cunnaway. The head of the Kanawha River. In his biography of Washington, Douglas S. Freeman concluded the Indians actually described the massacre of the family of Robert Foyle, which occurred on the Monongahela.

The Mouth of Yaughyaughgane. The mouth of the Youghiogheny River, now the site of McKeesport, Pennsylvania.

Queen Alliquippa. An Indian queen who has been identified as either a Seneca or a Delaware.

PAGE 23

Belvoir. The home of Colonel William Fairfax on the Potomac River.

PAGE 27

Marquiss Duguisne. A printer's error for Duquesne, the French Governor-General. The name is spelled correctly on the original manuscript.

A Note to the Reader

George Washington's journal was printed in Williamsburg by William Hunter in 1754. Eight copies of that original edition are known to exist. This facsimile of the Hunter edition has been printed from the copy owned by Colonial Williamsburg.

Those who would like to read more widely into the background and circumstances of Washington's journey will find a detailed commentary in Volume One of Douglas S. Freeman's biography, *George Washington* (1948), pages 259-350. A competent study of the journey also appears in Hugh Cleland, *George Washington in the Ohio Valley* (1955) on pages 1-55. This book includes a facsimile of the London edition of the journal, also printed in 1754. Two recent books that deal with Washington's early years are: James T. Flexner, *George Washington: The Forge of Experience, 1732-1775* (1965); and Bernhard Knollenberg, *George Washington, The Virginia Period, 1732-1775* (1964). The Anglo-French rivalry in North America is the subject of Francis Parkman's two-volume classic, *Montcalm and Wolfe,* one of the monumental works in American history. A lively historical account of the great area drained by the Ohio River is in Richard E. Banta, *The Ohio* (1949).

THE JOURNAL OF MAJOR GEORGE WASHINGTON
was printed by the Meriden Gravure Company, Meriden,
Connecticut, for the Colonial Williamsburg Foundation,
Williamsburg, Virginia. The papers are Kilmory
Text and Williamsburg Book. Binding is by the
Tapley-Rutter Company, Moonachie, New Jersey.
Introduction and Notes are by
James R. Short and Thaddeus W. Tate, Jr.
Illustration and map are by
Richard J. Stinely